THE POWER OF DECISION

"And if it seem evil unto you to serve the Lord, choose you this day whom ye will serve….."

Joshua 24:15

By
Franklin N. Abazie

The Power of Decision

COPYRIGHT 2018 BY Franklin N Abazie
ISBN: 978-1-945-133-71-8
All right reserved. This book or any portion thereof may not be reproduced or used in any manner whatsoever without the express written permission of the publisher, except for the use of brief quotations in a book review. All Bible quotes are from King James Version and others as noted.

Published by: F N ABAZIE PUBLISHING HOUSE---
a.k.a,
Empowerment Bookstore:

That I may publish with the voice of thanksgiving and tell of all thy wondrous works. **Psalms26:7**

To order additional copies, wholesales or booking: Call the Church office (973-372-7518)
or Empowerment Bookstore Hotline 973-393-8518
Worship address:
343 Sanford Avenue Newark New Jersey 07106
Administrative Head Office address:
33 Schley Street Newark New Jersey 07112
Email:pastorfranknto@yahoo.com
Website www.fnabaziehealingministries.org
Publishing House: www.fnabaziepublishinghouse.org

This book is a production of F N Abazie
Publishing House.

A publication Arms of Miracle of God Ministries 2018
First Edition

CONTENTS

THE MANDATE OF THE COMMISSION..........iv

ARMS OF THE COMMISSION............................v

INTRODUCTION..viii

CHAPTER 1

1. Making the Right Decision 54

CHAPTER 2

2. The Will of God..67

CHAPTER 3

3. Prayer of Salvation..86

CHAPTER 4

4. About the Author..95

THE MANDATE OF THE COMMISSION

"THE MOMENT IS DUE TO IMPACT YOUR WORLD THROUGH THE REVIVAL OF THE HEALING & MIRACLE MINISTRY OF JESUS CHRIST OF NAZARETH.

I AM SENDING YOU TO RESTORE HEALTH UNTO THEE AND I WILL HEAL THEE OF THY WOUNDS, SAID THE LORD OF HOST."

ARMS OF THE COMMISSION

1) F N Abazie Ministries-Miracle of God Ministries (Miracle Chapel Intl)

2) F N Abazie TV Ministries: Global Television Ministry Outreach.

3) F N Abazie Radio Ministries: Radio Broadcasting Outreach.

4) F N Abazie Publishing House: Book Publication.

5) F N Abazie Bible School: also called Word of Healing Bible School (W.O.H.B.S)

6) F N Abazie Evangelistic Ass: Miracle of God Ministries: Global Crusade

7) Empowerment Bookstore: Book distribution.

8) F N Abazie Helping Hands: Meeting the help of the needy world wide

9) F N Abazie Disaster Recovery Mission: Global Disaster Recovery.

10) F N Abazie Prison Ministry: Prison Ministry for all convicts "Second chance"

Some of our ministry arms are waiting the appointed time to commence

FAVOR CONFESSION

Father thank you for making me righteous and accepted through the blood of Jesus Christ. Because of that, I am blessed and highly favored by God. I am the subject of your affection. Your favor surrounds me as a shield, and the first thing that people see around me is your favored shield.

Thank you that I have favor with you and man today. All day long people go out of their way to bless me and help me. I have favor with everyone that I deal with today. Doors that were once closed are now opened for me. I receive preferential treatment, and I have special privileges, I am Gods favored child.

No good thing will he withhold from me. Because of Gods favor my enemies cannot triumph over my life. I have supernatural increase and promotion. I declare restoration to everything that the devil has stolen from my life. I have honor in the midst of my adversaries and an increase in assets, especially in real estate and expansion of territories.

Because I am highly favored by God, I experience great victories, supernatural turnarounds, and miraculous breakthrough in the midst of great impossibilities. I receive recognition, prominence, and honor. Petitions are granted to me even by ungodly authorities. Policies, rules, regulations, and laws are changed and reverse on my behalf.

I win battles that I don't even have to fight, because God fights them for me. This is the day, the set time and the designated moment for me to experience the free favor of God, that profusely and lavishly abound on my behalf in Jesus name. Amen.

INTRODUCTION

"And if it seem evil unto you to serve the Lord, choose you this day whom ye will serve....." **Joshua24:15**

I may never meet you in person-one to one, but I am excited to meet you here. In deed I love the power of literature. It preserves the word of God in print. This small book, the power of decision is a book of life.

It is written, *"Have not I commanded thee? Be strong and of a good courage; be not afraid, neither be thou dismayed: for the Lord thy God is with thee whithersoever thou goest."* **Joshua1:9**

"Seek ye out of the book of the Lord, and read: no one of these shall fail, none shall want her mate: for my mouth it hath commanded, and his spirit it hath gathered them." **Isaiah34:16**

In this small book, I encourage you to make the right decision and at the right time.

"There is a way that seemeth right unto a man, but the end thereof are the ways of death." **Prover16:25**

"I call heaven and earth to record this day against you, that I have set before you life and death, blessing and cursing: therefore choose life, that both thou and thy seed may live." **Deut30:19**

Decisions are the platform for any great destiny in life. Shallow men think of luck, but smart men think of cause and effect.. Until you make the take the right step, you will never prevail. David said, *"Order my steps in thy word: and let not any iniquity have dominion over me."*

Decisions are the foundation for any great future in life. Every decision have power to affect our lives. As long as you make the wrong decision in life, you will never succeed. Come with me as revealed by the Holy Spirit the power to make the right decision and at the right time.

Happy Reading!

HIS DESTINY WAS THE CROSS….

HIS PURPOSE WAS LOVE…..

HIS REASON WAS YOU….

"For a just man falleth seven times, and riseth up again: but the wicked shall fall into mischief."

Proverb24:16

"And said to his servant, Go up now, look toward the sea. And he went up, and looked, and said, There is nothing. And he said, Go again seven times."

1king18:43

"And it came to pass at the seventh time, that he said, Behold, there ariseth a little cloud out of the sea, like a man's hand. And he said, Go up, say unto Ahab, Prepare thy chariot, and get thee down that the rain stop thee not."

1king18:44

Endurance Prayer Points

"If ye shall ask any thing in my name, I will do it.." **John14:14**

Holy Spirit of God frustrate and disappoint, every one that is against my life and family, in the name of Jesus.

Father Lord destroy every demonic networks and traps against my progress in life in the name of Jesus.

Fire of God, destroy every demonic projection and curses against my life and destiny in the name of Jesus.

Every spell and curses pronounced against my destiny, break, in the name of Jesus.

Hand of God cage every power militating against my rising in life, in the name of Jesus.

Power of God silent every voice raising a counter motion against my elevation, in the mighty name of Jesus.

Blood of Jesus neutralize every spirit of Balaam hired to hinder my life, ministry, and career, the name of Jesus.

Fire of God destroy every curse that I have brought into my life through ignorance and disobedience, break by fire, in the name of Jesus.

Ancient of day destroy every power harassing my ministry in the name of Jesus.

Father God deliver me from invincible forces militating against my life and destiny.

Power of God frustrate every coven and demonic network, designed to frustrate and hinder my success in life, in the name of Jesus.

I dismantle every strong hold designed to imprison my talent in the mighty name of Jesus.

I reject every cycle of frustration, in the name of Jesus.

Power of God paralyze every agent assigned to frustrate my life in the name of Jesus.

Finger of God, grant me supernatural speed against all my contenders in the name of Jesus.

By the blood of Jesus, I destroy every familiar spirit caging my life and career.

Fire of God arrest every demonic agents, assigned to police my destiny and marriage.

By the blood of Jesus, I proclaim no weapon fashioned against me shall ever prosper.

Holy Spirit of God break me through and forward in life in the mighty name of Jesus.

God, smash me and renew my strength, in the name of Jesus.

Holy Spirit, open my eyes to see beyond the visible to the invisible, in the name of Jesus.

Father Lord grant me strength and power in the name of Jesus.

O Lord, liberate my spirit to follow the leading of the Holy Spirit.

Holy Spirit, teach me to pray through problems instead of praying about, it in the name of Jesus.

Father Lord, deliver me from the false accusation in life, in the name of Jesus.

By the blood of Jesus, every evil spiritual padlock and evil chain hindering my success, be roasted, in the name of Jesus.

By the blood of Jesus I rebuke every spirit of spiritual deafness and blindness in my life, in the name of Jesus.

Father Lord, empower me to dominate the enemy of my destiny in the name of Jesus.

Jesus Christ of Nazareth, heal my infirmities in the name of Jesus.

Lord, anoint my eyes and my ears that they may see and hear wondrous things from heaven.

Father Lord, anoint me with power and authority to dominate all my enemies in the name of Jesus.

Fire of God roast every giant rising up against my life and career.

Holy Spirit of God destroy all my oppressors in the name of Jesus.

Angels of good new, bring my good news to me in the mighty name of Jesus.

Every strong man holding me down, lose your hold now in the name of Jesus.

I nullify every demonic prediction over my life in the name of Jesus.

By the blood of Jesus, I flush out every polluted deposit of the enemy in my life.

By the blood of Jesus, I paralyze every enemy of my promotion in the name of Jesus.

Father Lord, destroy any power tormenting my life that is not from you.

Holy Ghost fire, ignite the fire of revival in my life.

By the blood of Jesus, I declare victory over every conflicting trial.

By the Blood of Jesus, I command the arrest of every demonic spirit, militating against my life .

By the blood of Jesus, I proclaimed the blood of Jesus, over every device of the enemy.

By the blood of Jesus, I revoke stagnation and hardship over my life in the name of Jesus.

Holy Ghost fire, destroy every satanic arrangement in my life, in the name of Jesus.

Circular problems, assigned to my life, you will not prosper, backfire, in the name of Jesus.

Every satanic project, against my breakthrough, explode in the face of the enemy, in the name of Jesus.

Every dream of backwardness, go back to your senders, in the name of Jesus.

Any power, working round the clock, with dark powers, against my life, perish, in the name of Jesus.

Every household Cain, assigned to waste my Abel, you will not succeed, rush to your grave and die, in the name of Jesus.

Every domestic enemy, anointed by Satan, to terminate my life, terminate your own life, in the name of Jesus.

Anti-Christ power of my father's house, assigned to punish me, die, in the name of Jesus.

Every satanic contact of my father's house, hunting for my life, die, in the name of Jesus.

Every magician, astrologer and diviner, assigned against me, go back to your senders, in the name of Jesus.

Every evil progress, against my life, perish, in the name of Jesus.

Mid-night and mid-day arrows, fired at me, collide on the Rock of Ages and backfire, in the name of Jesus.

Every giant, occupying my promised land, lose your hold, in the name of Jesus.

By the power that silenced Sennacherib, I silence my adversaries forever, in the name of Jesus.

Every wicked altar, harboring my name and my picture, collide with thunder and die, in the name of Jesus.

Every affliction, targeted at me, explode in the hands of your owners, in the name of Jesus.

Every king Saul of my household, pursuing my David, die, in the name of Jesus

Satanic grave digger of my father's house, dig your own grave and enter into it, in the name of Jesus.

Any power that has joined witchcraft and occult group to attack me, thus saith the Lord, suffer not a witch to live, lose your life for my sake, in the name of Jesus.

Arrows of shame, disgrace, and mockery, fired into my life, backfire, in the name of Jesus.

Arrows of rise and fall, fired at me, expire, in the name of Jesus.

Every vulture of darkness, assigned to eat my flesh, go back to your senders, in the name of Jesus.

Every verdict of darkness, issued against me, backfire, in the name of Jesus.

Every dominant wicked power of my father's house, I bury you now, in the name of Jesus.

Every satanic traditional manipulation, assigned to remove my glory, fail, in the name of Jesus.

Any power, assigned to make me irrelevant in my generation, your time is up, die, in the name of Jesus.

Any power, giving me a deadline to die, fall down, and die on your own deadline, in the name of Jesus.

Every strange material and strange deposit, in my body, disappear now and go back to your senders, in the name of Jesus.

Every satanic payroll, where my enemies registered my name, I delete my name and substitute it with the names of the enemies, in the name of Jesus.

Any wicked hand, collecting evil against me, decay, and die, in the name of Jesus.

By the power that silenced Haman in favor of Mordecai, O Lord, let every power assigned against my existence, die, in the name of Jesus.

Any power assigned to manipulate my destiny, enough is enough, scatter, in the name of Jesus.

Every assembly of the wicked, delegated to destroy my destiny, scatter, in the name of Jesus.

Every ancient strongman, laboring to waste my efforts, my life is not your victim, expire, in the name of Jesus.

Every wicked mouth, sowing evil seeds against me, I command the seeds to catch fire, in the name of Jesus.

Every ancient gate, standing against my breakthroughs, scatter, in the name of Jesus.

I plug my destiny, into the mystery of divine favor, in the name of Jesus.

O thou that troubled the Israel of Mountain of Fire and Miracles Ministries, the God of Elijah shall trouble you today.

Every enemy, of the Miracles of God Ministries, scatter, in the name of Jesus.

O God, arise and uproot anything You did not plant inside the Miracles of God Ministries, in Jesus' name.

You fire of revival, fall upon Miracles of God Ministries, in the name of Jesus.

It is written, *"Do not be afraid of sudden terror; nor of the trouble from the wicked when it comes; for the Lord will be your confidence. And will keep your foot from being caught."* **(Proverb 3:26)**.

Therefore, O Lord, cover us and our loved ones from the activities of terrorists, in Jesus name!

It is written, *"Avenge me of my adversary."* **(Luke. 18:3)**.

Therefore, O Lord, arise and avenge us of all my adversaries in the name of Jesus!

It is written, *"They fought from the heavens; the stars from their courses fought against Sisera."* **(Judges. 5:20)**.

Therefore O heavens, fight for us in Jesus name!

It is written, *"I will purge the rebels from among you, and those who transgress against me; I will bring them out of the country where they dwell, but they shall not enter the land of Israel. They will know that I am the Lord."* **(Ezekiel. 20:38)**

Therefore, O Lord, purge and sanitize our household in the name of Jesus!

It is written, *"Then it was so, after all your wickedness – "woe, woe to you!" says the Lord God."* **(Ezekiel. 16:23)**

Therefore, woe unto all the vessels that the enemy is using to do us harm in the name of Jesus!

It is written, *"Behold therefore, I stretch out my hand against you, admonished your allotment, and gave you up to the will of those who hate you..."* **(Ezekiel. 16:27)**

Therefore, let our enemies be delivered into the hands of their enemies in Jesus name!

It is written; you shall be for fuel of fire; your blood shall be in the midst of the land. You shall not be remembered, for I the Lord have spoken (Ezekiel. 21:32)

Therefore, let all our spiritual enemies become fuel for divine fire in Jesus name!

It is written; then they will know that I am the Lord, when I have set a fire in Egypt and all her helpers are destroyed (Ezekiel. 30:8).

Therefore, O Lord, let all the helpers of our enemies be destroyed in the name of Jesus.

It is written, *"And the people to whom they prophesy shall be cast out in the streets of Jerusalem because of the famine and the sword; they will have no one to bury them – them nor their wives, their sons nor their daughters – for I will pour their wickedness on them."* **(Jer. 14:16).**

Therefore, O Lord, pour the wickedness of those who seek to destroy us upon their own heads in the name of Jesus!

It is written, *"Call together the archers against Babylon. All you who bend the bow encamp against it all around; let none of them escape. Repay her according to her work; According to all she has done, do to her; for she has been poured against the Lord, against the Holy one of Israel."* **(Jer. 50:29).**

Therefore, let all the hosts of the Lord turn against our spiritual enemies in Jesus name!

It is written, *"Let God arise, let His enemies be scattered; let those also who hate him flee before him."* **(Psalms. 68:1).**

Therefore, O God, arise and let all your enemies in our lives be scattered in Jesus name!

It is written, *"And He that searches the hearts knows what the mind of the spirit is, because He makes intercession for the saints according to the will of God."* **(Romans 8:27)**

Therefore, the intercessory prayers of Jesus, who is seated on the right hand of the throne of God, will not be in vain over our lives, in the name of Jesus.

It is written, *"The Lord is your keeper; the Lord is the shade at your right hand. The sun shall not strike you by day, nor the moon by night. The Lord shall preserve you from all evil; He shall preserve your soul. The Lord shall preserve our going out and our coming in from this time forth, and even forevermore."* **(Psalms. 121:5-8)**

Therefore, O Lord, spread your covering of fire and the blood of Jesus over us and our loved ones, in the name of Jesus.

Therefore, O God, arise and let all your enemies in our lives be scattered in Jesus name!

It is written, *"And He that searches the hearts knows what the mind of the spirit is, because He makes intercession for the saints according to the will of God."* **(Romans 8:27)**

Therefore, the intercessory prayers of Jesus, who is seated on the right hand of the throne of God, will not be in vain over our lives, in the name of Jesus.

It is written, *"The Lord is your keeper; the Lord is the shade at your right hand. The sun shall not strike you by day, nor the moon by night. The Lord shall preserve you from all evil; He shall preserve your soul. The Lord shall preserve our going out and our coming in from this time forth, and even forevermore."* **(Psalms. 121:5-8)**

Therefore, O Lord, spread your covering of fire and the blood of Jesus over us and our loved ones, in the name of Jesus.

It is written, *"Rejoice always, pray without ceasing, in everything give thanks; for this is the will of God in Christ Jesus for you."* **(1 Thess. 5:16:18)**.

Therefore, we thank you Father, for raising a spiritual shield over our loved ones and us. Thank you for giving us the heart for appreciating everything you are doing for us. Thank you for filling our hearts and our home with joy and peace that surpasses all understanding. Blessed be your name for all the answers to our prayers in the name of Jesus!

You are holy, holy, Lord God Almighty, who was and is and is to come, Amen!

O Lord, let our season of divine intervention appear in the name of Jesus!

O you gates in the heavenlies standing against our destiny, lift up your heads in the name of Jesus!

O you gates in the waters standing against our destiny, lift up your heads in the name of Jesus!

O you gates in the earth standing against our destiny, lift up your heads in the name of Jesus!

O you gates under the earth standing against our destiny, lift up your heads in the name of Jesus!

O God, arise and destroy every gate keeper assigned against our lives in the name of Jesus!

We break the backbone of every spirit of scarcity in our lives in the name of Jesus!

O Lord anoint our eyes to see divine opportunities in the name of Jesus!

Lord let every blindness to the treasures of our lives be cleared in the name of Jesus!

Let our divine helpers appear in the name of Jesus!

We declare, O Lord, that the rest of our lives will be better than the first part, in Jesus name!

We declare, O Lord that will overcome obstacles and defeat every enemy, in Jesus name!

We declare, O Lord that every blessing and promise that you put in our hearts will come to pass because this is our time for favor, in Jesus name!

We declare, O Lord that this is a new season of increase in our lives. We speak health, wisdom, creativity, divine connections, and supernatural opportunities. They are coming our way, in Jesus name!

We declare, O Lord that we choose faith over fear. We are victorious in faith, in Jesus name!

We declare, O Lord that that we are not just surviving, this is our time to thrive in prosperity, in Jesus name!

We declare, O Lord that we will believe that we have received in the spirit even though we do not see anything happening in the flesh, in Jesus name!

We declare, O Lord that our rewards are being transferred to us because we remain in faith, in Jesus name!

We declare, O Lord that doubt will not ruin our optimistic spirit, in Jesus name!

We declare, O Lord that we are prisoners of hope and get up every morning expecting your favor, in Jesus name!

We declare, O Lord that you will do amazing things in our lives, in Jesus name!

We declare, O Lord that we are closer to your abundant blessing than we think, our time has come, your promises will come to pass, in Jesus name!

We declare, O Lord that we will stay in an attitude of faith and expectation, in Jesus name!

We declare, O Lord that we are not worried, we know that you are our vindicator. It may seem to be taking a long time, but we will reap in due season if trust in you Lord, in Jesus name!

We declare, O Lord that you know the secret petitions our heart and we believe that they will come to fulfilment, in Jesus name!

We declare, O Lord that you will open new doors for us, in Jesus name!

We declare, O Lord that we will see your goodness, in Jesus name!

We declare, O Lord that this is our time to believe because favor is coming our way, in Jesus name!

We declare, O Lord that you have paved the way to abundant prosperity for us, prosperity more than we can every dream of or imagine, for your sake, in Jesus name!

We declare, O Lord that in your eyes our future is extremely bright, in Jesus name!

We declare, O Lord that we will rise higher and higher and see more of your favor and blessings and we will live the prosperous life you have in store for us, in Jesus name!

We declare, O Lord that we may have a lot of troubles, but we know that everything is going to be alright, in Jesus name!

We declare, O Lord that we have faith because we have put you first, in Jesus name!

We thank you, O Lord that our set time for favor is here, in Jesus name!

We declare, O Lord that our hour of deliverance has come, in Jesus name!

We declare, O Lord that there is no limit to what we can do, in Jesus name!

We declare, O Lord that there is no obstacle we cannot overcome, in Jesus name!

We declare, O Lord that that we have seen your accomplishments and they are good, in Jesus name!

We declare, O Lord that there is no challenge that is too great for us because you are with us, in Jesus name!

We declare, O Lord that you always succeed, in Jesus name!

We declare, O Lord that there is no financial difficulty or situation in our lives that is too great for you to resolve, in Jesus name!

We declare, O Lord that you are our Father Jehovah Jireh and that you own everything and you are our provider, in Jesus name!

We declare, O Lord that your promises declare that we are destined to live a victorious life, in Jesus name!

We declare, O Lord that we are your children, in Jesus name!

We declare, O Lord that the seeds of increase, success, and promotion are taking a new root; your favor will spring forth in our lives in a great way; we will see new seasons of blessings and new seasons of your favor. It's our time to have abundant faith, in Jesus name!

O Lord, it is written; according to your faith, it will be done unto you. Ps. 2:8 says *"ask me and I will give you the nations as your inheritance."*

Therefore, we ask you Lord to fulfil our highest hopes and dreams, in Jesus name!

We ask you this day, O Lord to give us our abundant blessing now, in Jesus name!

We dare to exercise our faith by asking you O Lord so that we may receive indeed, in Jesus name!

We thank you O Lord that for encouraging our faith, in Jesus name!

We declare, O Lord that this is our time for favor, in Jesus name!

We declare, O Lord that this is our time to prosper abundantly, in Jesus name!

We declare, O Lord that this is our time to have instant answers to prayer, in Jesus name!

We declare, O Lord that this is our time to ask and receive, in Jesus name!

We declare, O Lord that this is our time to thank you and testify for answered prayer, in Jesus name!

We declare, O Lord that we are blessed and that goodness and mercy are following us right now, in Jesus name!

We declare, O Lord that you favor is surrounding us like a shield – you prosper us even in the desert, in Jesus name!

We declare, O Lord that you have great things for us in the spirit and that you have already released favor into our prayers, in Jesus name!

We declare, O Lord that you are a great and Holy God, in Jesus name!

It is written; delight yourself in the Lord and he will give you the desires of your heart (Ps 37:4).

We therefore declare, O Lord that we delight in you because you are our Father God and because we are your children you have made us the head and not the tail. You want to take us to a new level of prosperity, in Jesus name!

We declare, O Lord that because we are your children, we are more than conquerors, in Jesus name!

We declare, O Lord that we are blessed and you supply all our needs. We have more than enough, in Jesus name!

We declare, O Lord that we have abundant favor indeed, in Jesus name!

We declare, O Lord that we are filled indeed with the presence of the Holy Spirit, in Jesus name!

We declare, O Lord that we have abundant faith indeed, in Jesus name!

We declare, O Lord that you have answered our prayers, in Jesus name!

We declare, O Lord that our debts are all paid up, in Jesus name!

We declare, O Lord that we are healthy, in Jesus name!

We declare, O Lord that we have no lack and that we have more than enough, in Jesus name!

We declare, O Lord that we are extremely blessed so much that we can bless your kingdom, in Jesus name!

We declare, O Lord that we are extremely blessed so much that we can bless others, in Jesus name!

We declare, O Lord that we have entered into an anointing of ease, in Jesus name!

We declare, O Lord that for every opportunity we have missed, every chance we've blown, you will turn the clock and bring bigger and better things across our path, in Jesus name!

We declare, O Lord that we will not settle for less than your best, in Jesus name!

Please restore the time that we have lost, O Lord that, in Jesus name!

Restore our victories, O Lord, in Jesus name!

Restore our lost joy, lost peace, lost health, lost insight, lost faith, lost dedication, and desire to please you, we declare, O Lord in Jesus name!

We declare, O Lord that you use what was meant for our harm to our advantage, in Jesus name!

We declare, O Lord that you are a faithful God, in Jesus name!

We declare, O Lord that you will blossom our lives in ways that we can never imagine, in Jesus name!

Chapter 1 - The Omnipotent Power of God

We know, O Lord that you will bless us abundantly, in Jesus name!

We know, O Lord that you will provide divine connections, in Jesus name!

We declare, O Lord that we are not suffering – we are blessed, in Jesus name!

We declare, O Lord that our difficulties will give way to new growth, new opportunities, and new vision, in Jesus name!

O Lord let us see your blessing bloom in our lives in ways we would never dreamt possible, in Jesus name!

We declare, O Lord that we will stay in faith, so that what was meant to stop us will not be a stumbling block but a stepping stone taking us to a higher level, in Jesus name!

We declare, O Lord that we are not ordinary, but we are children of the most-high God, in Jesus name!

We declare, O Lord that we created to rise above problems, in Jesus name!

We declare victory over strife O Lord, in Jesus name!

We declare, O Lord that no weapon formed against us shall prosper, in Jesus name!

We declare, O Lord that we are healthy and that no sickness shall live in us, in Jesus name!

We declare, O Lord that triumph is our birthright, in Jesus name!

We declare, O Lord that our setbacks are simply setups for greater comebacks that will place us to be better than we were before, in Jesus name!

We declare, O Lord that with you all things are possible, in Jesus name!

We declare, O Lord that we are in agreement with you. We know you have supernatural favor in store for us. You have supernatural opportunities, supernatural healing, and supernatural restoration, in Jesus name!

Chapter 1 - The Omnipotent Power of God

We declare, O Lord that you want to do unusual things in our lives, in Jesus name!

We declare, O Lord that in faith, we have expectation deep in our spirits, in Jesus name!

We declare, O Lord that this will not be a survival year but a supernatural year in which you will abundantly come through for us, in Jesus name!

We believe, O Lord that you have come through for us, in Jesus name!

We declare, O Lord that because we hope in you, we will not be put to shame, in Jesus name!

We declare, O Lord that your word is right and true, you are faithful in all you do, in Jesus name!

We declare, O Lord that you are our refuge and strength, an ever present helper, in Jesus name!

We declare, O Lord that we will cast our cares on you and you will sustain us, you will never let the righteous fall, in Jesus name!

We declare, O Lord that you are the strength of our hearts and our portion forever, in Jesus name!

We declare, O Lord that you are our dwelling, therefore, no harm will befall us, and no disaster will come near our tent, in Jesus name!

We declare, O Lord that you are our refuge and our fortress, in Jesus name!

We declare, O Lord that you will command your angels concerning us to guard us in all our ways, in Jesus name!

We declare, O Lord that even in darkness the light will dawn for us, in Jesus name!

We declare, O Lord that your word is eternal and stands firm in the heavens, in Jesus name!

Chapter 1 - The Omnipotent Power of God

We declare, O Lord that your faithfulness will continue throughout all generations, in Jesus name!

We declare, O Lord that you will keep us from harm; you will watch over our lives; you will watch over our coming and our going both now and for evermore, in Jesus name! (Psalms. 121)

Thank you O Lord for the assurance that you are watching over us even when we sleep, in Jesus name! (Psalms. 13:5-6)

We declare, O Lord that you will drive those that do evil away from us and that you will protect us from their influence, in Jesus name! (Ps. 66:1-4)

We will shout with joy to you O Lord, we will sing the glory of your name and make your praise glorious. How awesome are your deeds! So great is your power that your enemies cringe before you, in Jesus name!

We declare, O Lord that that we will give you thanks for you answered us, in Jesus name! (Psalms. 118:21)

We declare, O Lord that we will praise you with all our hearts; before the gods we will sing your praise. We will bow down towards your Holy temple and will praise your name for your love and your faithfulness, for you have exalted above all things, your name, and your word, in Jesus name! (Psalms. 138:1-3)

Chapter 1 - The Omnipotent Power of God

"Finally, brethren, whatsoever things are true, whatsoever things are honest, whatsoever things are just, whatsoever things are pure, whatsoever things are lovely, whatsoever things are of good report; if there be any virtue, and if there be any praise, think on these things."

Phil4:8

I have decided to follow Jesus song

I have decided to follow Jesus;
I have decided to follow Jesus;
I have decided to follow Jesus;
No turning back, no turning back.
The world behind me, the cross before me;
The world behind me, the cross before me;
The world behind me, the cross before me;
No turning back, no turning back.
Though none go with me, still I will follow;
Though none go with me, still I will follow;
Though none go with me, still I will follow;
No turning back, no turning back.
My cross I'll carry, till I see Jesus;
My cross I'll carry, till I see Jesus;
My cross I'll carry, till I see Jesus;
No turning back, no turning back.
Will you decide now to follow Jesus?
Will you decide now to follow Jesus?
Will you decide now to follow Jesus?
No turning back, no turning back.

Chapter 1 - The Omnipotent Power of God

"Trust in the LORD with all thine heart; and lean not unto thine own understanding." **Proverbs 3:5**

"If any of you lack wisdom, let him ask of God, that giveth to all [men] liberally, and upbraideth not; and it shall be given him." **James 1:5**

"For I know the thoughts that I think toward you, saith the LORD, thoughts of peace, and not of evil, to give you an expected end." **Jer 29:11**

"And thine ears shall hear a word behind thee, saying, This [is] the way, walk ye in it, when ye turn to the right hand, and when ye turn to the left." **Isaiah 30:21**

"And this is the confidence that we have in him that, if we ask any thing according to his will, he heareth us:" **1 John 5:14**

"Where no counsel is, the people fall: but in the multitude of counsellors there is safety." **Proverbs 11:14**

"Whether therefore ye eat, or drink, or whatsoever ye do, do all to the glory of God." **1 Corinthians 10:31**

Trust and Obey

When we walk with the Lord
In the light of His Word,
What a glory He sheds on our way;
While we do His good will,
He abides with us still,
And with all who will trust and obey.
Trust and obey,
For there's no other way
To be happy in Jesus,
But to trust and obey.

Not a shadow can rise,
Not a cloud in the skies,
But His smile quickly drives it away;
Not a doubt or a fear,
Not a sigh or a tear,
Can abide while we trust and obey.

Not a burden we bear,
Not a sorrow we share,
But our toil He doth richly repay;
Not a grief or a loss,
Not a frown or a cross,
But is blest if we trust and obey.

Chapter 1 - The Omnipotent Power of God

But we never can prove
The delights of His love,
Until all on the altar we lay;
For the favor He shows,
And the joy He bestows,
Are for them who will trust and obey.

Then in fellowship sweet
We will sit at His feet,
Or we'll walk by His side in the way;
What He says we will do;
Where He sends, we will go,
Never fear, only trust and obey.

CHAPTER 1
Making the Right Decision

"And if it seem evil unto you to serve the Lord, choose you this day whom ye will serve; whether the gods which your fathers served that were on the other side of the flood, or the gods of the Amorites, in whose land ye dwell: but as for me and my house, we will serve the Lord." **Joshua 24:15**

The first decision we all have to make in life, is a decision to serve the Lord. By this I mean, a decision to give our life to Jesus Christ. Unless you live for "Christ" crisis has power to prevail in your life.

Have you given your life to Jesus Christ?

It is written, *"But seek ye first the kingdom of God, and his righteousness; and all these things shall be added unto you."* **(Mathew 6:33)**.

I believe the first decision in life for any adult is a decision to live for Jesus Christ.

A decision to turn from our wicked ways and embrace love, truth, honesty, compassion, righteousness, humility, and the fear of the Lord. A decision to love unconditionally and treat people nice and right. That is the totality of the gospel of Jesus Christ.

We live in a terrible time. Hell is real and eternity is certain. The bible says, *"For what shall it profit a man, if he shall gain the whole world, and lose his own soul?"* **(Mark8:36)**.

"For what is a man profited, if he shall gain the whole world, and lose his own soul? or what shall a man give in exchange for his soul?" **(Mathew 16:26)**.

The first step to any great decision, is a decision to live and serve the Lord Jesus. *"Have you accepted Him today?"*

Although there are other relevant decision for us to make in life, the complexity of our life depends upon our first decision for Christ.

Chapter 1 - Making the Right Decision

YOU MUST BE BORN AGAIN?

I like to warn you before you make any wrong move. Righteousness have no measured value to equal it. God is looking for honest men and women who are determined to live for Him.

Talking about Abraham we were told *"And he believed in the Lord; and he counted it to him for righteousness."* **Genesis15:6**.

Righteousness means *"right standing with God."* Abraham was a typical example of men that lived for God. The bible says *"Righteousness exalteth a nation: but sin is a reproach to any people."* **(Proverb14:34)**.

The bible said that Herold fear John because he was a just man. *"For Herod feared John, knowing that he was a just man and an holy,..."* **Mark6:20**.

Every time you live a crooked life, you end up in vanity.

Just like the bible says *"wealth gotten by vanity shall diminish."*

"Wealth gotten by vanity shall be diminished: but he that gathereth by labour shall increase." **Proverb13:11**

God is not an Author of Confusion

If God is not leading you, then the devil is leading you. We were told, *"There is a way that seemeth right unto a man, but the end thereof are the ways of death."* **Proverb14:12**

"There is a way that seemeth right unto a man, but the end thereof are the ways of death." **Proverb16:25**

Every time God lead's them it ended well. *"And they thirsted not when he led them through the deserts: he caused the waters to flow out of the rock for them: he clave the rock also, and the waters gushed out."* **Isaiah48:21**.

Chapter 1 - Making the Right Decision

Listen to me, indecision, and delayed decisions leads to poverty in life. The right decision is the key to a great future. The truth is that; the ability to make the right decision is influenced by numerous factors including our personality. A lot of people have trouble with making the right choices because of their environment.

"And when he came to himself, he said, How many hired servants of my fathers have bread enough and to spare, and I perish with hunger! I will arise and go to my father, and will say unto him, Father, I have sinned against heaven, and before thee."
Luke15:17-18

Like the scripture above, I believe it is never too late to make the right decision in life. Making the right decisions sometimes means making a commitment to a choice and sticking with it, but often there is an opportunity to find out something new, either about oneself, or about another person or topic.

Having an opportunity to find out something can make decisions fun. Unfortunately people who have trouble with decision-making see opportunity as another trap.

The Prodigal Son from the scripture below was not embarrassed or ashamed to return to his Father.

Some of us who have failed with a given opportunity have trouble with commitment. The fact that you failed in your last attempt does not make you a failure. The Prodigal son saw a great opportunity in his own father house.

The best way to make a decision is by deciding. Every time you leave a decision to fate, environment, or to time, it does not always end well. Most people who are afraid of failure need to work on worst-case scenarios. What is the worst that could happen if my choice is wrong? Can anything be salvaged?

Chapter 1 - Making the Right Decision

Since part of the problem is the fear of humiliation at making a mistake, that also needs to be taken into account. If any bad choice, no matter how minor, leads to extreme humiliation, then the feelings of humiliation need to be part of the decision process. Often people who feel humiliation at being wrong tend to feel an exaggerated version of feelings. Thus, there is no such thing as a little humiliation. Any error brings on a load of self-negation and anger.

Dealing with humiliation as a consequence of a mistake means that few decisions are made. It doesn't help the person to point out to them how silly their humiliation is, or that they needn't feel this way. They already do. What they need instead is a way to decrease the negative feeling associated with decisions.

This requires a two-pronged approach. One prong is to have them make tiny decisions they already can do, and take time to feel the positive feelings associated with having made the choice (not with the result, just with making the choice. It's important to disconnect the feeling from the result).

The second prong is to prepare for bad feelings. How can negative feelings be decreased or tolerated until they dissipate? One way to prepare is to rehearse doing a thing and having it turn out well. Using script, sort of like in a play, the person and a helpful other can rehearse what the choice is, how to make it and how to feel about making it. If the results are negative, they can rehearse alternatives and feelings that would go with them.

If results are positive, they rehearse feeling positive about having gone through the process that leads to the good decision. Another aspect of this is replaying past decisions and dissecting them for cues about when feelings of humiliation or anger started. Rehearse the choice as if the feeling were less intense. Over time, with practice, the feelings will become less intense.

Some people have trouble with making decisions because they have trouble setting priorities. To them every choice looks about the same, and there is no way to tell what makes one better than another. Some of these folks then impulsively pick a choice.

Chapter 1 - Making the Right Decision

This results in poor judgment since they pick the choice that stood out in some way - it was novel or interesting or highly stimulating but not necessarily helpful. Others can't pick anything at all because they feel they have no basis for picking. Both groups of people need help in learning how to weigh pros and cons, look at practical aspects, see the longer-term advantages, or note the big picture.

It might seem easier sometimes to think about life in the olden days or life in a monastery in some religion in which possessions are few, but few of us would really choose to go there for long. We'd miss all our favorite things, all those things we once chose. Besides maybe our goal ought to be not having fewer choices, but allowing others more. That we can do by making good decisions about how we use our world and the things in it for all our benefit.

Wouldn't it be great if there was a great hand from heaven pointing to the right decision? We can procrastinate as long as possible, but eventually the time will come when a decision has to be made.

Decisions are tough because of the consequences that linger afterwards. What Bible verses can help in the days of tough decisions?

Ask for Wisdom in Prayers

"If any of you lacks wisdom, you should ask God, who gives generously to all without finding fault, and it will be given to you" **(James 1:5)**.

We should always begin with asking God for wisdom. The wisdom that comes from the world brings a temporary relieve followed by more frustration. The wisdom from God brings peace and life even when it gets tough. When we pray in faith believing that God will give us wisdom to make the best choice, He responds and gives us more than what we need.

Search the scriptures of God

The Holy Scripture is the compass of life for anyone who genuinely want divine guidance in life. Every time you search the scripture you give yourself a head's up into the next decision before you.

Chapter 1 - Making the Right Decision

Be still before God

"Be still before the Lord and wait patiently for him; do not fret when people succeed in their ways, when they carry out their wicked schemes" (Psalm 37:7).If you are in a rush, you will miss the voice of the Holy Spirit. If you desire God to lead you, then you must be still. It is written "Be still, and know that I am God: I will be exalted among the heathen, I will be exalted in the earth." **(Pslams46:10)**

Seek counsel from Godly people

"Walk with the wise and become wise, for a companion of fools suffers harm" **(Proverbs 13:20)**

Everyone can have an opinion on what is the best decision for you. However, it's important to screen out the voices and hear from those who walk closely with God. Pray and ask the Lord to reveal His wise servants to you. You will recognize the Spirit of God within them because their advice leans heavily on the truths of God's word without fear, anxiousness, or presumption.

Have faith and trust in God

"Trust in the Lord with all your heart and lean not on your own understanding; in all your ways submit to him, and he will make your paths straight" (Proverbs 3:5-6). The truth of the gospel of Jesus is, never trust in anyone; man boy girl or woman. We were told *"Thus saith the Lord; Cursed be the man that trusteth in man, and maketh flesh his arm, and whose heart departeth from the Lord."* **Jer17:5**

Admit your weakness and limitations to God

"For we do not have a high priest who is unable to empathize with our weaknesses, but we have one who has been tempted in every way, just as we are—yet he did not sin" **(Hebrews 4:15)**

We must come to a place of recognizing our utter dependency on God. Many times tough decisions bring us to see both the good and bad within us.

We can't make excuses for our sins; rather we must immediately confess them and seek the Lord's cleansing. There's no shortcut to dealing with sin—it must be dealt with quickly or it can pollute our choices.

Be open and available to the revelation of God's will

"Submit yourselves, then, to God. Resist the devil, and he will flee from you" **(James 4:7)**

In the decision making process, the Lord can bring new revelations that seem out of the norm for us. Yet if we are really to walk by faith, we must keep our hearts open to other possibilities. God is above our thoughts and plans—He can move mountains of problematic choices and make a way for us. Every time we breathe in His will and breathe out our own, there is an opportunity for miracles.

It's time to make the right decision for your life

If you have been un-decisive about a particular decision, it's time for you to pray about it and make the right decision for your life.

CHAPTER 2
The Will of God

"Then said I, Lo, I come in the volume of the book it is written of me, to do thy will, O God." **Hebrew 10:7**

So many Christians have been frustrated in an attempt to foil the will of God. Christians desire God's will. Jesus himself said,

"He that hath my commandments, and keepeth them, he it is that loveth me: and he that loveth me shall be loved of my Father, and I will love him, and will manifest myself to him." **John 14:21**

The will of God is not for any to perish, but for all to come into repentance. Christians seek God's will to fulfil the commandment of the scriptures.

Although we all as Christians approve doing of God word as commanded by the Holy Scripture in our life, putting it into practice is the most difficult task for a lot of people.

It is written, *"For this is the will of God, even your sanctification, that ye should abstain from fornication:"* **1theo4:3**

James said, *"Be doers of the word, and not hearers only, deceiving yourselves"* **(James 1:22)** and we joyfully do whatever God wills.

In my opinion, I believe the will of God is the will of man. Often we narrow our choices in life. The truth is that, the will of God is our assignment on earth. It is our calling in life. There is something you were created and designed for.

"A man's gift maketh room for him, and bringeth him before great men." **Proverb18:16**

The will of God is the will of man. We are told" The Spirit itself beareth witness with our spirit, that we are the children of God."Romans8:16.

What is the will of God?

"...but if any man be a worshipper of God, and doeth his will, him he heareth." **John9:31**

Chapter 2 - The Will of God

"For whosoever shall do the will of God, the same is my brother, and my sister, and mother." **Mark3:35**

"For so is the will of God, that with well doing ye may put to silence the ignorance of foolish men:" **1peter2:15**

Often a lot of us mistake the truth. *"God will is our will."* Often our heart is so fix on certain things that no persuasion whatsoever will deter us from pursuing it. If that has ever happened to you, I like you to do the following. Pray again about it and allow the Holy Spirit to lead you.

HOW TO FOLLOW GOD'S WILL FOR OUR LIFE:

Knowing the will of the Father is the most ultimate thing any believer can desire in life. If you must know what Father God is saying then you must do the following:

DREAM BIG

Do you have a plan for your future? If you do not have any plan you are not going anywhere. God want us to dream big in life. If you have no dream, how can you decide?

One man decide by himself to become a beggar in life. All he wanted was to eat the crumb that fell from the rich man's dinner table.

"And there was a certain beggar named Lazarus, which was laid at his gate, full of sores, And desiring to be fed with the crumbs which fell from the rich man's table: moreover the dogs came and licked his sores." **Luke16:20-21**

"Now unto him that is able to do exceeding abundantly above all that we ask or think, according to the power that worketh in us." **Ephesians3:20**

If you do not dream big you have reduced your seize in life. *"One man said that your seize determine your rise."*

Chapter 2 - The Will of God

PLAN AHEAD

For the most part, we do not plan ahead. God kind of wisdom demands that *"we see ahead, plan ahead, and go ahead."* If you have not plan you cannot decide.

PRAYER

A prayer less person is anyone open to the attacks of the devil. If you do not pray, you are vulnerable to sickness, disease and all the assaults of the devil.

It is written, *"And he spake a parable unto them to this end, that men ought always to pray, and not to faint;"* **Luke18:1**

You cannot fulfill God's will for your life accidentally.

God's will for our life is divine. It doesn't come to pass through fate or by accident.

It is written, *"For whom he did foreknow, he also did predestinate to be conformed to the image of his Son, that he might be the firstborn among many brethren. Moreover whom he did predestinate, them he also called: and whom he called, them he also justified: and whom he justified, them he also glorified."* **Romans 8:29-30**

Chapter 2 - The Will of God

CONCLUSION

"...but as for me and my house, we will serve the Lord." **Joshua24:15**

The first step in any decision making in life is a decision for the Lord Jesus. Have you accepted the Lord Jesus?

Are you saved?

"Therefore if any man be in Christ, he is a new creature: old things are passed away; behold, all things are become new." **2Cor5:17**

What must I do to determine my divine visitation?

To determine divine visitation you must be born again. The word says as many as received him, to them gave He power to become the sons of God. Even to them that believe on his name.

To qualify for divine visitation do the following sincerely;

1) Acknowledge that you are a sinner and that He died for you. **Rom3:23**.

2) Repent of your sins. **Acts 3:19, Luke13:5, 2Peter3:9**

3) Believe in your heart that Jesus died for your sin. **Romans10:10**

4) Confess Jesus as the Lord over your life. **Romans10:10, Acts2:21**

Now repeat this Prayer after me

Say Lord Jesus, I accept you today, as my Lord and my savior, forgive me of my sins wash me with your blood. Right now, I believe, I am sanctified, I am save, I am free, I am free from the Power of sin to serve the Lord Jesus. Thank you Lord for saving me. Amen.

Chapter 2 - The Will of God

I am inviting you to come and worship with me every Wednesday, Friday, Saturdays, and Sundays.

MIRACLE OF GOD MINISTRIES

343 Sanford Avenue, Newark New Jersey 07106

Website: www.fnabaziehealingministries.org

Below is our worship service schedule;

Worship Service

Wednesdays: 7:00pm-9:00pm –Bible study

Fridays: 10:45pm-1:00am Encounter Night

Saturdays: 10:45am-12:45pm Financial Empowerment

Sundays: 10:45am-12:45pm Prophetic Signs & Wonders Service

WISDOM KEYS

Every Productive Society is a society heading to the top

Millions of Nigerians run away from Nigeria, very few Nigerians stay in Nigeria.

My decision to return Nigeria is the will of God for my life

My short coming in America after 18 years, trained me to be wise, to think, reflect and reason appropriately.

If you train your mind to reason it will train your hands to earn money.

It is absurd to use the money of the heathen to build the kingdom of the living God.

Every Ministry reveals its agenda and goal either at the beginning or at the end. Be careful of your life it is your first Ministry.

The average American mind is conditioned for a continual quest to get new things and (discard the former) and throw away old things.

Chapter 2 - The Will of God

When I considered well, my BMW jeep became my initial deposit for the work of the ministry in Nigeria

Everyone is waiting for you to change your mind until you change your thinking nothing changes around you.

Multiple academic degrees in other discipline gave me the chance to think, reflect and reason

What so everyone are thinking and reflecting at the moment reveals you to the time and the now factor

All events and intents are the product of precise thought processes, accurate reason every event is designed for a designated timeline

Wisdom is your ability to think, to create and invent. If you can think wise enough you will come out of penury

The distance between you and success is your creative ability to think reason and reflect accurate.

Success is the result of hard work, commitment resolve and determination learning from past mistakes and failing.

If you organize your mind you have organized your life and destiny.

There is a thin line between success and failure. If you look above and beyond you are on your way to success.

Wealth is your ability to think, power is your ability to reason and success is your ability to be informed.

If you can make use of your mind by thinking and reasoning God will make use of your life and destiny.

Think and Be Great

Reflect, Reason, think and be great

Famous people are born of woman

Chapter 2 - The Will of God

That you will make it is your intention; that you will survive is your resolve, that you will succeed with changes is your determination, personal efforts and hard work.

No man was born a failure. Lack of vision is the end product of failure.

Working with mental patients encourages and aspire me to be a productive observant and dedicated to my assignment.

Successful people are not magicians, it is the will power combined with hard work, and determination and a resolve to succeed that make them succeed.

In the unequivocal state of the mind, intention is not a location or a position it is the state of the mind.

So many people think that they think. The mind is used to think reflect and reason. You will remain blind with your eye open until you can see with your mind by thinking.

There is no favoritism in accurate and precise calculation

Although knowledge is power, information is the key and gateway to a great future.

It will take the hand of God to move the hand of man.

With the backing of the great wise God, nothing will disconnect you from your inheritance.

As long as you have wisdom and understanding of God, Satan and evil cannot manipulate your life and destiny.

You have come this far by yourself judgment and decision you have made in the past, now lean and listen to God for another dimension of greatness.

Great people are common people it is extra ordinary effort and the price of sacrifice that produces greatness.

As a mental direct care worker I saw a great pastor and a motivational speaker within myself.

Menial job does not reduce your self-worth, until you resolve to achieve greatness see greatness in all you do; you will never count in your community

Chapter 2 - The Will of God

The principle of Jesus will solve your gambling and addiction problems

The man of Jesus will lead you into heaven,

Everyone have their self-appraisal and what they think about you. Until you discover yourself other opinion about you will alter the real you.

Supervisors and directors are just a position in the chain of command in a work place. Never allow your supervisor hierarchy to alter your opinion about yourself.

Everyone can come out of debt if they make up their mind.

That I am not a decision maker at work does not diminish my contribution to my world.

Although it appears like it was a poor decision to accept a direct care employment at a psychiatric hospital as I reflect of my nine years of experience, it became apparent that I have learnt and experienced enough for my next assignment.

Self-encouragement and determination is a resolve of the heart.

The Power of Decision by Franklin N. Abazie

If you are determined to make a difference, and do the things that make a difference you will eventually make a difference.

Good things do not come easy

Short cuts will cut your life short.

Those who look ahead move ahead.

Life is all about making an impact. In your life time strive to make an impact in your community.

Make friends and connect with people who are moving ahead of you in life.

If you can look around well you have come a long way in your life, made a lot of difference and realized a lot of success in life.

If you are my old friend, hurry up to reach out to me before I become a stranger to you.

Everything I am blessed with inspirations from God, that change my definition and interpretation of the world around me.

I thought I was stagnant and lonely until I looked around and noticed my children running around and my wife cooking.

Chapter 2 - The Will of God

At 40 I resigned my Job to seek the Lord forever.

My ministry took a drastic rise to the top when the wisdom of God visited me with knowledge and understanding.

You will be a better person if you understand the characteristics of your personality – your mood swings attitudes and habits.

It is the seed of love you sow into the heart of a child and a woman that you reap in due time.

Love is not selfish, love share everything including the concealed secrets of the mind.

As long as you have a prayer life and a bible; you will never feel lonely, rejected and idle in the race of life.

When good friends disconnect from you, let them go, they might have seen something new in a different direction.

Confidence in yourself and in God is the only way to bring you out of captivity

Never train a child to waste his/her time.

The mind is the greatest assets of a great future.

You walk by common sense run by principles and fly by instruction.

Those who fly in flight of life fly alone.

Up in the air you are alone. No one can toll you accept the compass of knowledge and information

I have seen a tolling vehicle I have seen a tolling ship I have never seen a tolling airplane.

I exercise my judgment and make a decision every minute of the day.

Decisions are crucial, critical and vital with reference to your future.

So many people wish for a great future. You can only work towards a great future.

Your celebrity status began when you discovered your talent. What are you good at? Work at it with all commitment.

Prayers will sustain you but the wisdom of God will prosper you.

When I met Oyedepo, his teachings changed my perspective, but when I met Ibiyeomie; His teaching changed my perception.

Chapter 2 - The Will of God

I will be successful in ministry if only I concentrate and focus my energy in the work of the ministry.

It took the late Dr. Vincent Pearle Norman's book to open my mind towards kingdom success.

CHAPTER 3
PRAYER OF SALVATION

"Neither is there salvation in any other: for there is none other name under heaven given among men, whereby we must be saved." **Acts4:12**

The first decision is to be born again. A decision for Christ.

To be saved we must be born again!

The word says as many as received him, to them gave He power to become the sons of God. Even to them that believe on his name.

To qualify for divine visitation do the following sincerely,

1) Acknowledge that you are a sinner and that He died for you. **Rom3:23.**

2) Repent of your sins. **Acts 3:19, Luke13:5, 2Peter3:9**

3) Believe in your heart that Jesus died for your sin. **Romans10:10**

4) Confess Jesus as the Lord over your life. **Romans10:10, Acts2:21**

Now repeat this Prayer after me

Say Lord Jesus, I accept you today, as my Lord and my savior, forgive me of my sins wash me with your blood. Right now, I believe, I am sanctified, I am save, I am free, I am free from the Power of sin to serve the Lord Jesus. Thank you Lord for saving me. Amen.

I adjure you to watch the Spirit of God bear witness with your Spirit confirming His word with signs following. The word says The Spirit itself beareth witness with our spirit, that we are the children of God.

Chapter 3 - Prayer of Salvation

MIRACLE CARE OUTREACH

"...But that the members should have the same care one for another" **1cor12:25**

We are all members of the body of Christ. Jesus commanded us to love our neighbor as ourselves. This includes caring for one another as a member of one body. True love is expressed in caring and giving. The word says for God so Love He gave....

Reach out to someone in need of Jesus, help someone in crisis find Christ. Look out and prove your love to Jesus by caring and inviting your friends and associates to find Jesus the Healer.

Invite your friends to our Home Care Cell Fellowship (Miracle chapel Intl Satellite fellowship) In the USA at 33 Schley Street Newark New Jersey 07112.

If you are in Nigeria—**MIRACLE OF GOD MINISTRIES**

A.K.A"MIRACLE CHAPEL INTL"
Mpama –Egbu-Owerri Imo state Nigeria.

(Home Care Cell fellowship Group). We meet every Tuesday at 6:00pm-7:00pm.

LIFE IS NOT ALL ABOUT DURATION BUT ITS ALL ABOUT DONATION

What does the above statement mean?....

"Life consists not in accumulation of material wealth.." **Luke12:15.**

"But it's all about liberality....meaning- what you can give and share with others." **Proverb11:25.**

When you live for others--You live forever- because you out live your generation by the legacy you live behind after you depart into glory to be with the Lord. But when you live to yourself - you are reduced to self—you are easily forgotten when you die and depart in glory.

Permit me to admonish you today to live your life to be a blessing to a soul connected to you today.

Chapter 3 - Prayer of Salvation

I want you to know that so many souls are connected and looking up to you, and through you so many souls will be saved and rescued from destruction. Will you disciple someone today to find Jesus Christ?

"As a genuine Christian; it is your duty to evangelize Jesus Christ to all you meet on your way. Jesus is still in the healing business-Jesus is still doing miracles from time of old to now.

Therefore tell someone about Jesus Christ today, disciple and bring them to Church."

John 1:45 Philip findeth Nathanael....

Please to prove the sincerity of your love for God today; please become a soul winner. The dignity of your Christianity is hidden in your boldness to proclaim and evangelize Jesus Christ to all you meet on your way.

There is a question mark on the integrity of your Christianity until you become a life soul winner. Invite someone to join us worship the Lord Jesus this coming Sunday.

MIRACLE OF GOD MINISTRIES

PILLARS OF THE COMMISSION

We Believe Preach and Practice the following,

1) We believe and preach Salvation to every living human being

2) We believe and preach Repentance and forgiveness of sins

3) We believe and preach the baptism of the Holy Spirit and Spiritual gifts

4) We believe and teach the Prosperity

5) We believe and preach Divine Healing and Miracles (Signs &Wonder)

6) We believe and preach Faith

7) We believe and Proclaim the Power of God (Supernatural)

8) We believe and Proclaim Praise& Worship to God

9) We believe and preach Wisdom

10) We believe and preach Holiness (Consecration)

11) We believe and preach Vision

12) We believe and teach the Word of God

13) We believe and teach Success

14) We believe and practice Prayer

15) We believe and teach Deliverance

This 15 stones form the Pillars of Our Commission.

Become part of this church family and follow this great move of God.

MY HEART FELT PRAYER FOR YOU

It is my vision to spread the word of God in print. It is also my vision for you to come to the knowledge of Christ Jesus.

I love desire for you to meet God through one of our books, video's, or other related materials. I will love to hear of your testimonies and encounter with the Lord Jesus. I love for you to take a few minutes and write me a note below.

REV FRANKLIN N ABAZIE

MIRACLE OF GOD MINISTRIES

33 SCHLEY STREET NEARK NEW JERSEY 07112

OR AT OUR WORSHIP ADDRESS AT

MIRACLE OF GOD MINISTRIES

343 SANFORD AVENUE

NEWARK NEW JERSEY 07106

Now let me Pray for you:

Father I thank you for hearing me always. Even now oh God, let us experience you free Spirit of power, sound mind and wisdom. In Jesus Mighty Name.

Make up your Mind

For unless you make up your mind, whatever I have been saying from the first page to this point makes no sense. I encourage you to make up your mind.

Believe God and believe in yourself that you will succeed. I like you to believe God, regardless of the prevailing challenges facing you. I want you to pray about it, and believe that you will succeed.

CHAPTER 4
ABOUT THE AUTHOR

Rev Franklin N Abazie is the founding and Presiding Pastor of Miracle of God Ministries with headquarters in Newark, New Jersey USA and a branch church in Owerri- Imo State Nigeria. He is following the footsteps of one of his mentors, Oral Roberts (Healing Evangelist) of the blessed memory.

The Lord passed Oral Roberts healing mantle two days before he went to be with the Lord at age 91 into the hand of healing evangelist-Rev Franklin N Abazie in a vision.

In all his services the Power and Presence of God is present to heal all in his audience. He is an ordained man of God with a Healing Ministry reviving the healing and miracle ministry of Jesus Christ of Nazareth.

Pastor Franklin N Abazie, is called by God with a unique mandate:

"THE MOMENT IS DUE TO IMPACT YOUR WORLD THROUGH THE REVIVAL OF THE HEALING & MIRACLE MINISTRY OF JESUS CHRIST OF NAZARETH.

I AM SENDING YOU TO RESTORE HEALTH UNTO THEE AND I WILL HEAL THEE OF THY WOUNDS. SAID THE LORD OF HOST"

He is a gifted ardent Teacher of the word of God who operates also in the office of a Prophet, generating and attracting undeniable signs & wonders, special miracles and healings, with apostolic fireworks of the Holy Ghost.

He is the founding and presiding senior Pastor of this fast growing Healing ministry.

He has written over 86 inspirational, healing and transforming books covering almost all aspect of divine healing and life. He is happily married and blessed with children.

BOOKS BY REV FRANKLIN N ABAZIE

1) Commanding Abundance
2) The outcome of faith
3) Understanding the secret of prevailing prayers
4) Understanding the secret of the man God uses
5) Activating my due Season
6) Overcoming Divine Verdicts
7) The Outcome of Divine Wisdom
8) Understanding God's Restoration Mandate
9) Walking in the Victory and Authority of the truth
10) Gods Covenant Exemption
11) Destiny Restoration Pillars
12) Provoking Acceptable Praise
13) Understanding Divine Judgment
14) Activating Angelic Re-enforcement
15) Provoking Un-Merited Favor
16) The Benefits of the Speaking faith
17) Understanding Divine Arrangement

18) Understanding Divine Healing
19) The Mystery of Endurance
20) Obeying Divine Instructions
21) Understanding the Voice of God
22) Never give up on Hope
23) The prevailing Power of faith
24) Understanding Divine Prosperity
25) The Reward of Prayer
26) Covenant Keys to Answered Prayers
27) Activating the Forces of Vengeance
28) Put your faith to work
29) Where is your trust?
30) The Audacity of the Blood of Jesus
31) Redeeming Your Days
32) The force of Vision
33) Breaking the shackles of Family Curses
34) Wisdom for Marriage Stability
35) Overcoming prevailing challenges
36) The Prayer solution
37) The power of Prayer
38) The Effective Strategy of Prayer
39) The prayer that works
40) Walking in Forgiveness
41) The power of the grace of God

42) The Power of Persistence
43) Overcoming Divine verdicts
44) The audacity of the blood of Jesus.
45) The prevailing power of the blood of Jesus
46) The benefit of the speaking faith.
47) Fearless faith
48) Redeeming Your Days.
49) The Supernatural Power of Prophecy
50) The companionship of the Holy Spirit
51) Understanding Divine Judgement
52) Understanding Divine Prosperity
53) Dominating Controlling Forces
54) The winners Faith
55) Destiny Restoration Pillars
56) Developing Spiritual Muscles
57) Inexplicable faith
58) The lifestyle of Prayer
59) Developing a positive attitude in life.
60) The mystery of Divine supply
61) Encounter with the Power of God
62) Walking in love
63) Praying in the Spirit
64) How to provoke your testimony

65) Walking in the reality of the Anointing
66) The reality of new birth
67) The price of freedom
68) The Supernatural power of faith
69) The intellectual components of Redemption
70) Overcoming Fear
71) Overcoming Prevailing Challenges
72) My life & Ministry
73) The Mystery of Praise

MIRACLE OF GOD MINISTRIES

NIGERIA CRUSADE 2012

MIRACLE OF GOD MINISTRIES
NIGERIA CRUSADE 2012

MIRACLE OF GOD MINISTRIES

NIGERIA CRUSADE

2012

MIRACLE OF GOD MINISTRIES

NIGERIA CRUSADE

2012

www.ingramcontent.com/pod-product-compliance
Lightning Source LLC
Chambersburg PA
CBHW021156080526
44588CB00008B/361